THE REAL PRINCESS DIARIES

By Grace Norwich

Scholastic Inc.

Library of Congress Cataloging-in-Publication Data available

ISBN 978-0-545-84937-1

10 9 8 7 6 5 4 3 2 1   15 16 17 18 19

Printed in the U.S.A. 40
First edition, September 2015

Book design by Paul Banks

PRINCESS PROFIILES AND MORE

REAL ROYALS 4

ROYAL TALK 5

HATSHEPSUT, PHARAOH OF EGYPT 8

THEODORA, EMPRESS OF THE BYZANTINE EMPIRE 12

MARY TUDOR, PRINCESS OF ENGLAND 16

ELIZABETH TUDOR, PRINCESS OF ENGLAND 20

ROYAL WEDDINGS 24

MARIE ANTOINETTE, PRINCESS OF HAPSBURG 28

VICTORIA, PRINCESS OF ENGLAND 32

CIXI, EMPRESS DOWAGER OF CHINA 34

SARAH FORBES BONETTA, AFRICAN PRINCESS 36

ROYAL PETS 38

VICTORIA KA'IULANI, PRINCESS OF THE KINGDOM OF HAWAII . . . 40

ANASTASIA NIKOLAEVNA, GRAND DUCHESS 44

ELIZABETH II, PRINCESS OF THE UNITED KINGDOM 46

GRACE KELLY, PRINCESS OF MONACO 50

NOT-SO-ROYAL DUTIES 54

UBOLRATANA RAJAKANYA, PRINCESS OF THAILAND . . . 56

DIANA, PRINCESS OF WALES 58

MASAKO, PRINCESS OF JAPAN 62

RANIA, PRINCESS OF JORDAN 64

FASHION QUEENS 66

VICTORIA, PRINCESS OF SWEDEN 68

KEISHA OMILANA, PRINCESS OF NIGERIA 70

KATE, DUCHESS OF CAMBRIDGE 74

THEODORA, PRINCESS OF GREECE AND DENMARK 78

ROYAL HAIRDOS 80

AMEERAH AL-TAWEEL, PRINCESS OF SAUDI ARABIA . . . 82

SIKHANYISO, PRINCESS OF SWAZILAND 86

SIRIVANNAVARI, PRINCESS OF THAILAND 88

BEATRICE AND EUGENIE, PRINCESSES OF YORK 90

PRINCE CHARMING 94

REAL ROYALS

L ots of little girls dream about being princesses. But real-life royalty isn't all tiaras and terrific clothes. Throughout history, royal women have been subjected to all sorts of unpleasantness. Luckily, today's aristocracy doesn't have to worry about beheadings, arranged marriages, or too-tight corsets. Still, they have their own pressures. There is the constant public scrutiny and an impossibly high standard they must try to live up to even though, under the gowns and jewels, real princesses are just real people. Like Princess Sikhanyiso of Swaziland, who studied digital communications at Sydney University, they go to school. They are ambitious, like Princess Ameerah Al-Taweel of Saudi Arabia, who advocates for women's rights in the Middle East. They work, like another English princess, Eugenie, who moved to New York City for her career. And like Princess Ubolratana Rajakanya of Thailand, who lost her son in the 2004 tsunami that swept the region, they experience tragedy.

Check out these princess profiles of the past and present to find out just what it means to live the royal way.

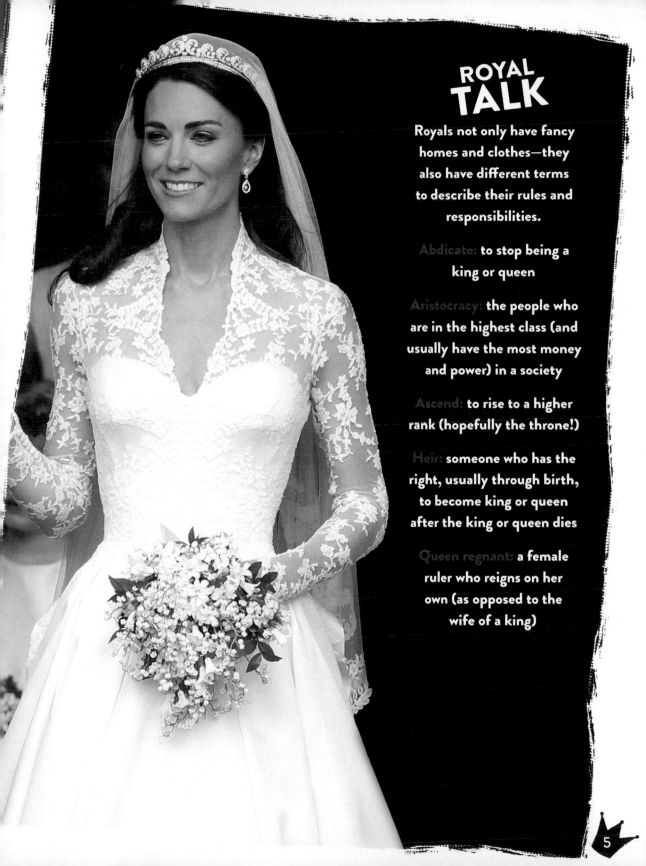

ROYAL **TALK**

Royals not only have fancy homes and clothes—they also have different terms to describe their rules and responsibilities.

Abdicate: to stop being a king or queen

Aristocracy: the people who are in the highest class (and usually have the most money and power) in a society

Ascend: to rise to a higher rank (hopefully the throne!)

Heir: someone who has the right, usually through birth, to become king or queen after the king or queen dies

Queen regnant: a female ruler who reigns on her own (as opposed to the wife of a king)

THE PRINCESSES

PHARAOH OF EGYPT
HATSHEPSUT

The Royal Life

Hatshepsut was only twelve years old when she married Tuthmosis II, who was the son of her father's second wife—her half brother. That wasn't unusual in their culture and time, and the couple had a girl named Neferure. When Hatshepsut's husband died around 1479 BCE, she officially ruled for her stepson Thutmosis III (the son of one of her husband's concubines), who was only an infant. The idea was that he would become the king once he came of age, but after a few years Hatshepsut decided to declare herself pharaoh. This was unheard of. In the 1,500 years before her, there had only been two or three other female pharaohs.

ROYAL RUNDOWN

LIVED:
c. 1508 BCE – 1458 BCE

HOMETOWN:
Thebes, Egypt

REGAL BEGINNINGS:
Although technically Hatshepsut couldn't become the heir to the throne of her father, King Tuthmosis I, because she was a girl, she became one of the strongest of the few women to rule over Egypt as pharaoh.

ROYALLY
COOL FACTS

When artists painted or sculpted Hatshepsut, she demanded to be portrayed as a man with big muscles and the false beard worn by other pharaohs.

Hatshepsut loved perfume—who doesn't?—and when she was buried, her nails were painted with red and black polish.

Hatshepsut accomplished a ~~P9-DCR-623~~ reign. Thanks to her, Egypt gained gold, ebony, leopard skins, ivory, wood, wild animals, and incense through trade routes she established. She discovered that the incense frankincense, when scorched, could be used as eyeliner! And she supervised hundreds of architectural projects throughout the realm, making her one of the most accomplished builders in Ancient Egypt. Now, that's progress.

EMPRESS OF THE BYZANTINE EMPIRE
THEODORA

The Royal Life

Theodora came from a poor family, and because of this she had a lot of jobs before she met Justinian. She danced, acted, spun wool, and more to make ends meet. By the time she married Justinian in 525, she also had a young child, which was pretty shocking to many. Two years later, her husband was crowned emperor. As empress, Theodora fought for better rights for women and better laws to protect them in situations such as divorce and kidnapping.

ROYAL RUNDOWN

LIVED:
c. 497 CE – June 28, 548 CE

HOMETOWN:
Constantinople, Byzantine Empire

REGAL BEGINNINGS:
Married to the Byzantine emperor Justinian I, who was also known as "the Last of the Romans" for his attempt to reconquer all the land of the original Roman Empire, Theodora was greatly involved in her husband's political decisions and wielded a lot of power for a woman at that time.

A Byzantine coin featuring Empress Theodora

Empress Theodora and her entourage

ROYAL ACHIEVEMENTS

Theodora understood what it was like to live in a society that didn't respect people like her; of course, she gained respect with her title. But that wasn't enough for the woman who would become known as one of the most powerful in Western history. Because she didn't have a privileged childhood, Theodora knew that if she wanted something, she had to work for it. And when it came to empowering women, that's exactly what she did. A feminist more than a thousand years before that was even a word, she created new laws that protected women against violence of all sorts and helped to remedy unfairness in society. For example, she created a house where former prostitutes who had no chance for marriage could live safely. These radical reforms led to a lot of people hating her. But what did she care? Simply put, Theodora ruled!

ROYALLY
COOL FACTS

Theodora's father was the bear keeper at the
Hippodrome (stadium) of Constantinople.
After he died when Theodora was five,
her mom married another animal keeper.

Empress Theodora urging Emperor Justinian to act against a mob of citizens

PRINCESS OF ENGLAND
MARY TUDOR

The Royal Life

Although Mary Tudor was the first queen to rule England in her own right rather than through marriage to a king, life was never easy for her. When Mary was just seventeen, she refused to give official approval for her parents' annulment—which would not only end their marriage but also Mary's status as a princess. Eventually, Mary, known for her stubborn personality, was forced to sign the papers. After that, her life changed drastically. She was no longer allowed to see or speak to her mother. After remarrying two more times, Mary's father, King Henry VIII, finally got his wish: the birth of a son. Edward VI became the heir to the throne a little earlier than expected, at just nine years old, after his father died. Edward's reign was also short, since he died of tuberculosis five years later. That's where Mary enters the picture. The Duke of Northumberland, in a plot to marry his son to King Henry's grandniece and make her queen, captured Mary so she wouldn't ascend the throne. But Mary wasn't going to let anything stand in the way of her becoming queen, and she escaped! During her reign, from 1553 until her death in 1558, Mary ruled with strength of conviction. She even went so far as to banish her half sister, Elizabeth, to the same castle her mother was sent to, in order to make sure Elizabeth couldn't succeed her as queen. (Mary never forgave Elizabeth for being the daughter of her dad's second wife, Anne Boleyn, whom she called "the Midnight Crow.") This was one area where she couldn't get her way. Mary, who wed the Emperor of Spain's son Phillip so she could have an heir, was never able to have a child. With no other choice, Mary had to leave Elizabeth as her successor.

ROYAL ACHIEVEMENTS

Mary I with her husband, Phillip II of Spain

Although there was controversy over the matter, Mary was the first woman to successfully call dibs on England's throne, and fought through the rest of her life to secure that title. She won over crowds with her speeches, especially regarding her religion, Catholicism, which was severely suppressed under the official English Protestant Church. However, what followed is not something to praise or consider an achievement. In her attempt to restore the Catholic Church in England, she ordered the execution of around three hundred Protestants in three years—many of whom were burnt at the stake. This gruesome and vicious plan didn't end Protestantism, but only served to earn her the nickname "Bloody Mary."

ROYALLY COOL FACTS

By her father's orders, Mary was very well educated, especially for a girl at the time. She had private tutors and studied Latin and French, among other subjects.

Despite her wishes to be buried near her mother, Mary is buried at Westminster Abbey near her half sister Elizabeth with an inscription, which translates to: "Partners both in throne and grave, here rest we two sisters, Elizabeth and Mary, in the hope of the Resurrection."

ROYAL RUNDOWN

LIVED:
February 18, 1516 – November 17, 1558

HOMETOWN:
Greenwich and London, England

REGAL BEGINNINGS:
Mary was a royal from the start.
Born Princess of Wales to parents
King Henry VIII and Queen Catherine,
she was crowned queen after the death of
her father and then her brother.

PRINCESS OF ENGLAND
ELIZABETH TUDOR

The Royal Life

Even though she was born a princess, life was no ball for Elizabeth, who was only two years old when her father banished her from court and beheaded her mother! Living in a castle apart, with servants that King Henry VIII ordered be "ancient and sad," the little girl asked, "How haps it . . . that yesterday I was my Lady Princess and today I am only Lady Elizabeth?" Unfortunately, that wasn't the last time Elizabeth's family would send her away. When her half sister, Mary, who wanted to reestablish Catholicism in England, became queen, she imprisoned the Protestant Elizabeth in the Tower of London. Eventually, Elizabeth was released, and she became queen after Mary's death.

ROYALLY COOL FACTS

Elizabeth was fluent in six languages: French, Greek, Latin, Spanish, Welsh, and English!

The very year Sir John Harrington invented the flush toilet, 1591, Queen Elizabeth had one installed in her home.

ROYAL RUNDOWN

LIVED:
September 7, 1533 – March 24, 1603

HOMETOWN:
Greenwich and London, England

REGAL BEGINNINGS:
When Elizabeth was born to King Henry VIII and his new wife, Anne Boleyn, the law of the land stipulated that she take over the title Princess of Wales previously held by her half sister, Mary Tudor.

Elizabeth's mother,
Anne Boleyn

Elizabeth's father,
King Henry VIII

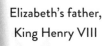

Procession of Queen Elizabeth and her court

ROYAL ACHIEVEMENTS

When Elizabeth became Queen of England in 1558, at the age of twenty-five, she ushered in a golden age of English history that spanned her forty-five-year reign. During this period, known as the Elizabethan Age, many advances were made in trade, exploration, and the arts. A very intelligent and educated woman, Elizabeth had studied history, math, geography, astrology, Greek, and Italian as a child. So it's no wonder that she cheered on her country's traders, mariners, writers, and painters. Only two years into her reign, she granted the East India Company a charter to import exotic goods like tea, silk, and salt from Asia. This powerful organization would go on to account for half of all trading in the world and lay the foundations for the British Empire. A lover of the arts, Elizabeth was a patron of theater and poetry who helped creative geniuses like William Shakespeare flourish. She was as independent and shrewd in her personal life as she was in her public one. By choice, Queen Elizabeth stayed a single lady until she died on the throne at the age of seventy.

ROYAL WEDDINGS

From their residences to daily responsibilities, every aspect of a royal's life is outsized—so why not their wedding day? The jewels are bigger, the trains on the gowns longer, and of course the price tag for the whole affair much, much larger. See how crazy it is when royalty says, "I do!"

MARIE ANTOINETTE AND LOUIS-AUGUSTE

May 16, 1770

Thousands of regular people gathered in the gardens of Versailles on the royal couple's wedding day. They filled the nearby roads with carriages, and rivers with boats. They had begun arriving as early as dawn to make sure they could be a part of the festivities. Of course, they didn't get to see the prince in his suit of gold fabric studded with diamonds, the princess in her white gown, or the two exchanging vows in the palace's royal chapel. But the gardens were the next best thing. Food and drink were distributed around the fountains of wine for anyone wishing to toast the royal family! The king had planned a magnificent fireworks display to cap off the day's events, but it had to be postponed because of a terrible thunderstorm. Not a great omen.

The Royal Chapel at Versailles

GRACE KELLY AND PRINCE RAINIER III

April 19, 1956

The press around the world dubbed the event "the Wedding of the Century," but the bride herself jokingly referred to it as "the Carnival of the Century." Whatever the term, about two thousand reporters showed up at Monaco Cathedral to cover the ceremony. And that's in addition to the fact that the wedding was already being filmed by MGM (as part of a deal she made with the studio to get out of her contract with them). Princess Grace, already known as a fashion icon from her days as a movie star, needed a showstopping dress. So she turned to a trusty source—the Academy Award–winning costume designer Helen Rose, who made the actress's costumes for the films *High Society* and *The Swan.* The gown of Brussels lace, seed pearls, and peau de soie was hand-sewn by nearly forty seamstresses in the MGM wardrobe department. The dress was a gift from the movie studio, but that wasn't the most lavish wedding present the royal couple received. The Greek shipping magnate Aristotle Onassis gave them a 147-foot yacht that the newlyweds took on their honeymoon!

In 2014, a thirty-three-year-old piece of Princess Diana and Prince Charles's wedding cake was sold in an auction for $1,375

LADY DIANA AND PRINCE CHARLES

July 29, 1981

Glass coach? Check. Tiara? Check. Wedding dress encrusted with ten thousand pearls and sequins, and a twenty-five-foot train? Done. The wedding of Princess Di and Prince Charles was truly something out of a fairy tale. Saint Paul's Cathedral was filled with 3,500 guests, and about a billion more around the world watched the couple exchange their vows on TV. The lavish wedding reception for Diana and Charles that night served breakfast food for dinner. Guests like Princess Grace of Monaco, the Empress of Iran, and the Crown Prince of Japan dined in Claridge's ballroom on sausages, baked beans, and scrambled eggs with smoked salmon.

CROWN PRINCE FELIPE OF SPAIN AND LETIZIA ORTIZ ROCASOLANO

May 22, 2004

The Crown Prince of Spain and the former news anchor tied the knot in Madrid's Almudena Cathedral, which was decorated for the ceremony with more than a million flowers. The 1,500 guests—including the UK's Prince Charles, Japan's Crown Prince Naruhito, and South African President Nelson Mandela—were well guarded by twenty thousand police officers. The wedding reception at the Pardo palace boasted one thousand bottles of Champagne and a wedding cake that was more than six feet tall. No wonder the entire wedding cost nearly $29 million!

KATE MIDDLETON AND PRINCE WILLIAM

April 29, 2011

No expense was spared for Kate and Will's wedding. The couple spent $80,000 on the cakes alone! Kate's gown—featuring hand-cut English and French Chantilly lace that was designed by Sarah Burton for Alexander McQueen—cost $400,000. Armies of florists covered Westminster Abbey and Buckingham Palace in flowers for about $800,000. But the largest expense by far wasn't the Jo Malone candles in Kate's favorite scents that were placed throughout the ceremony's venue, or the Aston Martin convertible the couple drove in after the reception. It was the security! Lucky for Kate's parents, the estimated $33 million in security costs was paid by the British taxpayers.

ROYALLY
COOL FACTS

Marie Antoinette was one of sixteen brothers and sisters!

The style maven never tied her corset, which she hated because of the metal underwire that jabbed her ribs.

She once bought a pair of diamond bracelets that cost as much as a Paris mansion.

PRINCESS OF HAPSBURG
MARIE ANTOINETTE

The Royal Life

Marie Antoinette was always over the top. When she moved to France in May of 1770 to marry the heir to the throne, she traveled with 57 carriages, 117 footmen, and 376 horses. Still, the feisty tomboy from Austria found the "French way" of living tough to swallow. Marie hated the court etiquette that dictated she dress with a group of noblewomen and court ladies watching—and eat her meals in front of a large crowd. Marie rebelled by adopting wild tastes in dresses, décor, and diversions. Instead of heavy, corseted dresses and rigid curled hair, she favored—shocker!—modern looks like thin muslin shifts with sashes and lightly powdered hair. When she wasn't ordering new clothes or expensive jewelry, Marie attended the opera or fancy balls—and she was crazy for gambling. While her country was in trouble—a bad harvest led to high food prices and shortages, and mobs rioted in the streets—Marie and her family, who continued to live it up in the luxury of Versailles, appeared corrupt and callous. The French people rebelled, and in 1792, Marie and the king were locked up in a medieval fortress in the center of Paris for being traitors. On October 16, 1793, less than a year after her husband was executed and two weeks before her thirty-eighth birthday, Marie was led to the guillotine. Before her beheading, the queen, who once donned the most elaborate gowns and towering hairdos, was paraded through Paris in a cart, wearing nothing more than a plain white dress.

Marie and her sisters, as children, performing in a ballet

ROYAL ACHIEVEMENTS

Marie Antoinette gets a bad rap in the history books. She did enjoy a lavish lifestyle and was more frivolous a queen than the times required, but many things people said about her during her time were simply gossip and nothing more. For example, it's generally accepted now that Marie did not say the famous line "Let them eat cake" in response to the news that Parisians were starving from a lack of bread. (It was actually most likely a quote from the Spanish princess Maria Theresa, who married Louis XIV about a hundred years earlier.) In fact, Marie Antoinette was calm right before her beheading because she said her "conscience is clear." Even as the executioner cut off her hair and tied her hands behind her with rope, she proved her strength. The priest on hand told her to have courage, to which Marie Antoinette eloquently replied, "The moment when my ills are going to end is not the moment when courage is going to fail me."

A calm Marie Antoinette before her execution

ROYAL RUNDOWN

LIVED:
November 2, 1755 – October 16, 1793

HOMETOWN:
Vienna, Austria

REGAL BEGINNINGS:
Born Maria Antonia Josepha Joanna, to Empress of Austria Maria Theresa and Holy Roman Emperor Francis I. She was an Austrian archduchess who was fourteen when she was sent to marry the future King of France, Louis XVI, and become France's last queen.

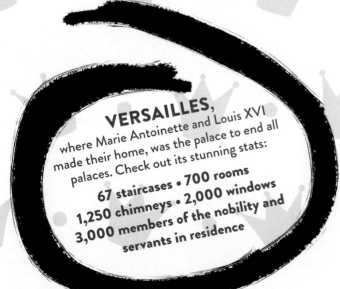

VERSAILLES, where Marie Antoinette and Louis XVI made their home, was the palace to end all palaces. Check out its stunning stats:

67 staircases • 700 rooms
1,250 chimneys • 2,000 windows
3,000 members of the nobility and servants in residence

PRINCESS OF ENGLAND
VICTORIA

ROYAL RUNDOWN

LIVED:
May 24, 1819 – January 22, 1901

HOMETOWN:
London, England

REGAL BEGINNINGS:
Alexandrina Victoria, born
at Kensington Palace, became
heir to the throne at only eight
months old when her father,
Edward, Duke of Kent,
whose three brothers
had no heirs, passed away.

The Royal Life

She might have been an English princess, but life was no picnic for young Victoria. When her father passed away, he left the family nothing but debts. Her family might have been poor (at least by royal standards), but Victoria's problems weren't about money. After her mother had British soldier Sir John Conroy take control over the family's finances, she also let him take a big role in raising young Victoria. Conroy's plan was to dominate the little princess so that he could control her when she became queen. He kept her away from the rest of the royal family, forbade her from going anywhere in the mansion alone, and disciplined her harshly—he tied her hands behind her back and made her stand in the dark on the stair landing! It's no wonder Victoria responded by throwing tantrums, refusing to bathe, and hurling a pair of scissors at her governess. (It's also no wonder that one of her first acts as queen was to throw Conroy officially out of her household.)

ROYAL ACHIEVEMENTS

Victoria's unhappy childhood makes it all the more remarkable that the woman who became queen in 1837 at the age of eighteen would rule longer than anyone else in British history, up until the current monarch, Elizabeth II. During the sixty-four years she sat on the throne, her country saw great cultural, economic, and technical progress—including the building of the London Underground. In 1851, Victoria opened the first world's fair, called the Great Exhibition, to display some of the new machines from the Industrial Revolution. Although she was greatly admired for her high standard of ethics, seven attempts were made on her life! The attacks only made Victoria more popular.

ROYALLY COOL FACTS

Princess Victoria was very good at painting with watercolors, something she did her whole life.

After becoming Empress of India in 1877 (India was part of the British Empire), Victoria learned how to write and speak Hindustani.

She was England's first ruler to live in Buckingham Palace, which she moved into only three weeks after she took the throne. (She couldn't get out of Kensington Palace fast enough!)

EMPRESS DOWAGER OF CHINA
CIXI

ROYALLY COOL FACTS

In 1906, she established the Peking Zoological Garden, which today holds 485 species and 4,000 animals, and was home to the world's very first giant panda bred in captivity.

Bandits blew up Cixi's tomb with dynamite in 1928 to steal her jewels and her teeth!

The Royal Life

Some have called Empress Dowager Cixi the most important woman in China's history. She certainly was the most powerful. She was the only wife of Xianfeng to have a son. She took advantage of the situation when her husband died in 1861 and her six-year-old boy, Tongzhi, inherited the throne. Cixi staged a palace coup. By various gruesome methods she rid herself of all the advisors her late husband had appointed, and put herself in charge.

ROYAL ACHIEVEMENTS

As the ruler of China for forty-seven years, she brought a third of the world's population from a medieval-style society into modern times. To do so she used any means necessary, including poisonings and beheadings (establishing a reputation for cruelty for herself). But Empress Dowager Cixi also did away with horrible customs such as foot-binding, introduced technology like electricity, squashed rebellions, oversaw wars with France and Japan, and much, much more.

ROYAL RUNDOWN

LIVED:
November 29, 1835 – November 15, 1908

HOMETOWN:
Beijing, China

REGAL BEGINNINGS:
The daughter of a government official, Cixi became a concubine of Emperor Xianfeng at age sixteen. This meant she didn't enjoy any of the rights or titles that came with marriage. It wasn't until their son turned one year old that the emperor made Cixi one of his many wives.

AFRICAN PRINCESS
SARAH FORBES BONETTA

ROYAL RUNDOWN

LIVED:
1843 – 1880

HOMETOWN:
Okeadan, Nigeria

REGAL BEGINNINGS:
When Sarah was born, Egabo tribal markings were cut into her face symbolizing that she was royalty in a West African dynasty. But when tragedy struck her young life, it was a British commander that saved her—in the name of Queen Victoria!—and gave her the name of Sarah Forbes Bonetta.

Full page image is a detail of this photo, obtained from the National Portrait Gallery in London

The Royal Life

When Sarah was five years old, Dahomian warriors attacked her village, killed her parents, and captured her. After spending two years as a captive, she was prepared for the ritual of honoring the ancestors of the Dahomey tribe with her life. One by one, prisoners like her were dropped into a pit. A British commander, Frederick Forbes—on an operation to end slavery—watched in horror. Sarah was only a child! Surely, Queen Victoria would not allow it if she were there! Forbes convinced the Dahomey king to release Sarah as a gift to Queen Victoria. Sarah then traveled back to England on Forbes's ship, the Bonetta (for which she was named), where she learned English from the sailors. When Sarah met Queen Victoria, the queen was impressed with Sarah's English and moved by her story. Sarah became the queen's protégé, receiving an excellent education, and forging a lifelong relationship between the two.

For a few years Sarah studied at an all girls school in Sierra Leone, like this one, where she excelled

Forbes referred to Sarah as "intelligent and good tempered," a description that would be echoed by others throughout her life, including the Queen. Sarah excelled in her studies and music. And whether she liked it or not, she was something of a celebrity. Still, her life was far from easy. She had endured incredible loss as a child, was moved about as a young girl, and as a young woman was pressured to marry a man she didn't love. But through it all, Sarah showed intelligence, graciousness, and strength. Now that's a princess!

Sarah rode in pony carts on the palace grounds with Queen Victoria's children.

Sarah named her first child Victoria to honor Queen Victoria, who became the child's godmother.

ROYAL PETS

Royals aren't too different from the average person; everyone needs a companion. Of course, when you have an enormous palace with acres of land for a pet to roam and lots of staff on hand to clean up the messes, why stick to boring old dogs and cats?

LIONS AND TIGERS

Cats were all the rage in ancient Egypt, most likely first domesticated during the Middle Kingdom period. Considered divine, they held a special position in the time of the pharaohs. The first cat name recorded in history was immortalized on the tomb of his owner, King Hana. In a carving found on the pharaoh's tomb, west of the Nile, the cat Bouhaki sits at his master's feet. Prince Tuthmosis buried his cat Ta-mit in its own sarcophagus! But Ramses II wasn't content with a pussycat as a pet. Instead, he had a lion and cheetahs. Cleopatra kept pet leopards purring on the steps of her throne.

Napoleon's wife, Josephine, kept exotic birds and animals brought to her by explorers. But her favorite pet of all was a female orangutan, which she dolled up in beautiful white dresses and let eat at the table!

AT YOUR SERVICE

For racing, Queen Elizabeth's father kept pigeons that were descendants of a gift originally given to his grandfather by King Leopold of Belgium. However, they also had the much more important mission of transporting messages during the First and Second World Wars. In 1940, one of the king's pigeons found an aircraft that had been reported missing. For his hard work and good services, they rewarded the little guy with a Dickin Medal in honor of his bravery. Here a young Elizabeth is ready to release another carrier pigeon.

A ROYAL'S BEST FRIEND

Many a princess has loved dogs. Marie Antoinette had many, many dogs, but her absolute favorite was her toy spaniel, Coco. Royal dogs have been more than just objects of affection. Empress Josephine used her pug, Fortune, to smuggle out secret messages while she was a prisoner at Les Carnes, where only the dog was allowed to visit. But there is, perhaps, no monarch more associated with dogs than Queen Elizabeth, who is famous for her corgis. After her father brought home her first corgi, Dookie, in 1933, it was love at first sight. Dookie was quickly followed by another, Jane, who gave birth to a litter of which the royal family kept two: Carol and Crackers. On the occasion of her eighteenth birthday, Elizabeth received—yup, you guessed it—another corgi, named Susan.

Prince William and Kate Middleton's cocker spaniel, Lupo, has his own children's book series, The Adventures of a Royal Dog.

Princess of the Kingdom of Hawaii
VICTORIA KA'IULANI

The Royal Life

Born to Princess Miriam Likelike (the king's sister) and Archibald Scott Cleghorn, a Scottish businessman, Ka'iulani had just the kind of childhood you'd expect a Hawaiian princess would have. She grew up on an idyllic estate in Waikiki that boasted ten gardens. She liked playing with her pet peacocks and riding her pony, Fairy, around town. Ka'iulani, often called "the island rose," could also play ukulele, dance hula, and—naturally—surf. But when she was eleven, tragedy marred her picture-perfect childhood. Her mother died, and two years later she was sent to boarding school in England, where she remained for years. It seemed like her mother's deathbed prediction was coming true. However, more heartbreak lay in store for Ka'iulani. In 1893, the Hawaiian monarchy was overthrown by an American-led revolt that planned to annex the islands to the United States.

ROYAL RUNDOWN

LIVED:
October 16, 1875 – March 6, 1899

HOMETOWN:
Waikiki Beach, Hawaii

REGAL BEGINNINGS:
Because her aunt and her uncle, the reigning King of Hawaii, were childless, Ka'iulani's birth meant she would one day inherit the throne. But as her mother, Princess Miriam Likelike, lay dying, she made the horrifying prediction that Ka'iulani would be sent away, never marry, and never become queen.

Ka'iulani was still in England when she heard the terrible news that her aunt, the queen, had abdicated, or formally given up the throne. Although she was only seventeen years old, she got on the first boat she could to New York to make the case for her country's independence. At that time, many thought of Hawaiians as "savages." But those prejudices about Ka'iulani were immediately wiped away when the beautiful, intelligent, and cultured young princess arrived in the United States. The press described her as "charming" and "fascinating." She was also determined.

She headed directly from New York to Washington, DC—to meet with the President of the United States! Persuaded by the enchanting and impassioned teenager, President Grover Cleveland put a stop to the annexation treaty being considered by the Senate. Unfortunately, the next American president, William McKinley, reversed course, and in 1898, Ka'iulani's beloved Hawaii became a part of the US. Ka'iulani, however, never fully gave up her fight. She worked to ensure that the Hawaiian people earned the right to vote. Alas, her life was cut tragically short when, only a year later, she became sick after riding her horse in a storm and died at the age of twenty-three.

"I, a poor, weak girl, with not one of my people near me and all these statesmen against me, have the strength to stand up for the rights of my people. Even now I can hear their wail in my heart, and it gives me strength."

—Victoria Ka'iulani

ROYALLY COOL FACTS

Robert Louis Stevenson—the author of *Treasure Island* and *The Strange Case of Dr. Jekyll and Mr. Hyde*, as well as a good friend of Ka'iulani's parents—called the princess "the island rose" in a poem he wrote for her titled "To Princess Ka'iulani."

Ka'iulani's namesake and hero was Queen Victoria, because the British monarch had consented to the restoration of the Kingdom of Hawaii's independence on July 31, 1843.

43

ROYAL RUNDOWN

LIVED:
June 18, 1901 – July 17, 1918

HOMETOWN:
Saint Petersburg, Russia

REGAL BEGINNINGS:
Anastasia's father was the last Russian tsar, Nicholas II.

GRAND DUCHESS ANASTASIA NIKOLAEVNA

The Royal Life

Grand Duchess Anastasia liked to joke around just as much as the next kid. Growing up in a tight-knit family that included three older sisters and one brother, she was infamous for her pranks around the house. She was always getting into trouble! It was not unusual to find the naughty grand duchess in just the right corner to trip an unsuspecting servant, or hiding in a cabinet to avoid a doctor's visit. Alas, the end of her life was no laughing matter. During a civil war led by Vladimir Lenin, when Communism replaced imperial rule in Russia, Grand Duchess Anastasia, at seventeen years old, and the rest of her family (even her beloved pet dog, Jimmy) were executed. For years it was believed that both Anastasia and her brother, Alexei, had survived. (One of the rumors was that the siblings were protected from the bullets that killed the rest of their family by jewels that had been sewn into their clothing to hide them.) Many women have claimed to be the Lost Grand Duchess. But in 2007, the ninety-year-old mystery was put to an end when, through DNA analysis, Anastasia's and her brother's remains were identified.

ROYALLY COOL FACTS

Anastasia was born in a palace with more than two hundred rooms.

She loved acting—especially pretending to be her friends and family. She also loved animals, like her dog, Jimmy. Sometimes she would act like a dog instead of a grand duchess!

Her feisty personality earned her the nickname of *shvibzik*, or "imp" in Russian.

ROYAL ACHIEVEMENTS

In addition to being a skilled reader, Grand Duchess Anastasia was a talented pianist who performed for her family at gatherings.

ROYAL RUNDOWN

BORN:
April 21, 1926

HOMETOWN:
London, England

REGAL BEGINNINGS:
Elizabeth, the longest-reigning
ruler in Britain's history, was
never even supposed
to be queen.

PRINCESS OF THE UNITED KINGDOM
ELIZABETH II

The Royal Life

As a little girl, Elizabeth was third in line to the throne of England, but no one ever thought she'd make it there. Her father, the Duke of York, wasn't supposed to be king. But her uncle abdicated the title and gave up the throne. (He married a divorced woman whose ex was still alive, which at the time wasn't permitted for the king by the Church of England.)

Elizabeth attended the coronation of her father, King George VI. Fifteen years later, she would follow in his footsteps. She was touring Kenya in 1952 with her husband, Prince Philip, when she got the news that her dad had died. The twenty-five-year-old princess immediately flew home, where Prime Minister Winston Churchill met her at the airport, because she was the country's new sovereign.

Queen Elizabeth II with her husband, Prince Phillip, after she was crowned on June 2, 1953

ROYAL ACHIEVEMENTS

No one has ruled over as great a period of social and technological change as Elizabeth—and she does it while never once losing the dignity befitting a British royal. The queen manages to keep up many of the monarchy's traditions even as she embraces modern changes. She not only supported ending the rule that only the eldest male child can succeed to the throne, but also offered to start paying taxes!

ROYALLY COOL FACTS

Princess Elizabeth was on the cover of *Time* magazine all by herself when she was just three years old.

The queen is the patron of six hundred charities—which means she gives them each a lot of money and support!

Her own personal bagpiper wakes her up every morning with fifteen minutes of blowing.

Queen Elizabeth has been gifted—from other countries—many, many exotic species, from Brazilian sloths to an African bull elephant. Because none of them would make very good pets, she donates them all to the London Zoo.

PRINCESS OF MONACO
GRACE KELLY

The Royal Life

When she was just twenty years old, Grace Kelly realized many a young girl's dream, signing with a big and glamorous film studio, MGM, and catapulting into Hollywood stardom. Grace worked with famous actors like Clark Gable, Ava Gardner, William Holden, and Cary Grant, starring in films like *Mogambo*, *The Country Girl*, and *To Catch a Thief*. In the 1950s, the Academy Award winner was the It Girl. Her natural elegance, exquisite features, and dancer's posture from years of studying ballet made her a style icon. She was as popular with her costars—like Jimmy Stewart and Frank Sinatra—as she was with her fans. But it wasn't enough for Grace Kelly to be Hollywood royalty. When she married Prince Rainier III, she became real, bona fide royalty: Grace, Princess of Monaco. The royal couple had three children. But tragically, her royal reign was cut short when on September 14, 1982 she was killed in a car accident in Southern France.

ROYAL ACHIEVEMENTS

Soon after becoming Princess of Monaco, Grace founded AMADE Mondiale, an organization that promotes the protection of children throughout the world, regardless of race or religion. She envisioned a world where every child could be free and safe.

Prince Rainer III and Princess Grace

ROYALLY COOL FACTS

Before becoming a princess, Grace performed in thirty-five live television dramas between 1950 and 1954.

Her family gave Prince Rainier a dowry of 2 million dollars for the marriage to go ahead. (Luckily, Grace's dad was a successful businessman!)

She was the very first actress to appear on a US postage stamp, issued in 1993.

ROYAL RUNDOWN

LIVED:
November 12, 1929 –
September 14, 1982

HOMETOWN:
Philadelphia, Pennsylvania

REGAL BEGINNINGS:
After years in the Hollywood spotlight, Grace married Prince Rainier III of Monaco in 1956.

NOT-SO-ROYAL DUTIES

While you probably aren't going to see Kate Middleton taking your order at a restaurant any time soon, many a royal has held down a job. (Even Kate worked as a part-time buyer for a London clothing company.) See what paid the bills before (or even while) they donned a tiara.

Cleopatra wrote a medical and pharmacological work called *Cosmetics*, which detailed several cures, including remedies for hair loss and dandruff.

Queen Silvia of Sweden was a flight attendant for a while, but she was working as an interpreter (she speaks six languages!) at the 1972 Summer Olympics in Munich when she met her husband, the future King Carl XVI Gustaf.

A television anchor and journalist, Letizia Ortiz Rocasolano met Prince Felipe of Spain in 2002 while reporting on an oil spill along the Galicia shoreline, where the prince was visiting to assess the ecological disaster.

Before she became Princess of Wales, Lady Diana was a kindergarten teacher.

Charlene Wittstock held another title before she married Prince Albert II and became Her Serene Highness The Princess of Monaco: member of the South African Olympic swimming team.

Grace Kelly's gorgeous granddaughter, Charlotte Casiragh, who is eighth in line to the throne of Monaco, has appeared in countless magazines as the face of Gucci's Forever Now campaign.

Princess Eugenie of York is putting her artistic sensibility to work at an art auction website in New York City.

Her Royal Highness Princess Lalla Salma was an engineer before marrying King Mohammed VI of Morocco in 2001.

Eugenie's sister, Princess Beatrice, spent a summer working at an investment capital firm, followed by an internship at Sony Pictures Europe headquarters in London.

BORN:
April 5, 1951

HOMETOWN:
Lausanne, Switzerland

REGAL BEGINNINGS:
The eldest daughter of Thailand's King Bhumibol Adulyadej and Queen Sirikit, she renounced her royal title to marry an American.

PRINCESS OF THAILAND
UBOLRATANA RAJAKANYA

The Royal Life

The Thai princess was in college at the prestigious Massachusetts Institute of Technology, when she fell in love with Peter Jensen. After the two married in 1972, Ubolratana was forced to give up her title of princess and decided to make the United States her home. She and her husband lived in California, where they raised three children. Not long after the couple divorced, however, Ubolratana moved back to Thailand in 2001. It was there that tragedy struck. During the 2004 tsunami that devastated much of Southeast Asia, her twenty-one-year-old son, Khun Poom, was killed while vacationing at a resort in Southern Thailand.

ROYAL ACHIEVEMENTS

Since returning to royalty, Princess Ubolratana has set her sights on helping the country that welcomed her home with open arms. She launched a major antidrug initiative called To Be Number One. The campaign aims to reduce drug abuse among teenagers by helping them develop their self-esteem and realize their full potential. The princess also started the Khun Poom Foundation, which has already granted over one hundred scholarships to children with autism and other learning disabilities.

ROYALLY COOL FACTS

Ubolratana's dad is the world's longest-serving monarch, having been Thailand's king for almost seventy years.

The princess is also a movie star! She played the lead role in the 2008 Thai film *Where the Miracle Happens*.

PRINCESS OF WALES
DIANA

The Royal Life

Although she became known as "the People's Princess," Diana Spencer was anything but ordinary. Starting with her wedding to Prince Charles at Saint Paul's Cathedral, which was viewed by a global television audience of over 750 million, Princess Di always seemed to be in the spotlight, whether it be her humanitarian efforts or her very public royal divorce from Prince Charles. Nonetheless, she handled her role with grace and warmth, being a devoted mother to her two sons, William and Harry, and volunteering her time and efforts to charities all over the world. Everything she touched became newsworthy, a blessing for the charities but an inevitable curse for Princess Diana. She tragically died in a car accident, which many believe to have been related to the paparazzi's fascination with Diana's every move. Just as the public had adored her in life, so was her death met with widespread mourning.

ROYAL ACHIEVEMENTS

While many princesses do some form of charity work (it sort of comes with the title), Princess Di was absolutely known for it. She raised money for organizations like the Red Cross and lent her fame to important issues such as the International Campaign to Ban Landmines. Princess Diana didn't just host fancy fund-raisers, she also met with those less fortunate. She visited war-torn countries like Angola and Bosnia to raise awareness about the dangers of landmines. Closer to home, she oversaw the Great Ormond Street Hospital for children. She was one of the first celebrities to be photographed touching a person with HIV, which went a long way in changing the public perception of AIDS. That moment was just one of the many compassionate things Princess Diana did throughout her life.

ROYAL RUNDOWN

LIVED:
July 1, 1961 – August 31, 1997

HOMETOWN:
Norfolk, England

REGAL BEGINNINGS:
Diana already had royalty in her family tree. She was a lady before she married Charles, Prince of Wales, in 1981.

Clockwise: Princess Diana, Prince Charles, Prince William, Prince Harry

The royal family, including Queen Elizabeth and the Queen Mother, at the christening of Prince Harry

Princess Diana, Prince Charles, Prince William

ROYALLY COOL FACTS

Diana was a talented singer and pianist, but she always wanted to be a ballerina. Unfortunately, she was considered too tall to pursue ballet professionally.

The princess visited many terminally ill patients in the hospital—completely unannounced—so the media would never know.

PRINCESS OF JAPAN
MASAKO

BORN:
December 9, 1963

HOMETOWN:
Tokyo, Japan

REGAL BEGINNINGS:
Masako became a princess after marrying Japan's Prince Naruhito.

The Royal Life

Masako had no plans of becoming a princess! The daughter of an ambassador, she attended Harvard, where she graduated magna cum laude with a degree in economics. This smart young woman was working in the Japanese foreign ministry when she met her husband, Prince Naruhito.

ROYAL ACHIEVEMENTS

Although many girls dream of becoming princesses, Masako was dedicated to her own plans, declining the first two proposals from Prince Naruhito. She was determined to have her own happily ever after (including a two-year program at Oxford University) before creating one together with him. The royal life, however, isn't as easy as most people imagine. For a long time, Masako was rarely seen in public. Under a lot of pressure to have a son who would be heir to the throne, the princess preferred the company of her family, which included her daughter, Aiko, born in 2001. In 2012, Masako bravely told the world that she had suffered from a stress-related illness, but that with the help of her family and doctors she was getting better. Indeed, shortly after her public statement, Masako made her first official trip overseas with her husband in over ten years!

The future bride and groom don traditional Japanese costumes before their wedding on June 2, 1993

ROYALLY COOL FACTS

As a child, Masako lived in Japan, Russia, and the United States.

When Masako took the Diplomatic Service Evaluation, she was one of just three women to pass (less than one quarter of the people who take it pass at all).

In high school, Masako was a star athlete and helped organize her school's girls softball team.

Queen Rania, the mother of four, cares deeply for all youth. That is why she founded the Queen Rania Teacher Academy, an organization dedicated to improving education in Jordan and the rest of the Middle East by offering teachers support, training, and the latest research. She is committed not only to improving public education in the Middle East, but also to addressing sensitive and taboo topics like child abuse, domestic violence, and honor killings.

PRINCESS OF JORDAN
RANIA

> *"No matter where we come from, what we look like, how we dress, or to whom we pray, when it comes to what makes us laugh or cry, when it comes to what we dream of for ourselves and for our children, when it comes to how hard we work each day, we are usually more alike than we are different."*
>
> —Queen Rania

The Royal Life

Rania attended school at the American University in Cairo. After she graduated with a major in business administration, she had jobs at Citibank and Apple. But her business career was interrupted when she met Prince Abdullah at a dinner party. Completely smitten with each other, the couple was engaged two months later, and married four months after that!

ROYAL RUNDOWN

BORN:
August 31, 1970

HOMETOWN:
Kuwait City, Kuwait

REGAL BEGINNINGS:
Rania became a princess after marrying Prince Abdullah. She then became queen at twenty-nine years old, when he became king.

The Jordan royal family, in 2000 (not shown, Prince Hashem bin Al-Abdullah, born in 2005)

ROYALLY COOL FACTS

Queen Rania has a Twitter account! Her username is @QueenRania.

She's not only a queen but also a children's book author.

FASHION QUEENS

Royals have always proven their power through fashion. Take Empress Dowager Cixi's silk robes embroidered with dragons that took hundreds of craftsmen to complete or Thai princess Sirivannavari Nariratana in head-to-toe couture sitting in the front row during Paris Fashion Week. From ancient times to present day, they have used clothing as a way to share something about their personalities and, in the process, set fashion trends that everyone wants to wear.

THE DUCHESS OF CAMBRIDGE

Kate likes to do her own shopping. She turned down the use of a royal dresser. Even so, the young royal has made best-dressed lists around the globe and put British fashion back on the map. But Kate doesn't only wear designer dresses that cost thousands of dollars. She regularly checks out the stuff in lower-priced stores like Topshop and Zara. When she makes a purchase at one of them, whatever she wears quickly sells out. The phenomenon is called "the Kate effect." Because of this, designers love to have Kate wear their clothes or accessories. As a result, loads of beautiful dresses, handbags, and shoes arrive at the palace each and every day. But the duchess can't accept anything for free, so each item is returned immediately to the sender (with a nice note—of course).

Marie Antoinette, who purportedly never wore anything twice, ordered three hundred gowns each year.

PRINCESS DEENA ABDULAZIZ

As the teenage daughter of a Saudi Arabian economist growing up in Santa Barbara, California, Princess Deena read *Vogue* religiously. Even so, she never imagined owning a world-famous designer boutique. But Deena, married to Prince Sultan Bin Fahad Bin Nasser Bin Abdulaziz, is the owner of Saudi Arabia–based boutique D'NA. She has been featured in *Vogue*, *Harper's Bazaar*, and many other fashion publications. Photographers are constantly snapping her for her amazing street style. All of this has translated into two wildly successful members-only boutiques in Riyadh and Doha that feature such deluxe items as a $7,691 Victoria Beckham sequin draped skirt, or a purple metallic backpack by Alexander Wang for $1,422.

QUEEN ELIZABETH

This British queen was the original fashionista, pulling styles from all over Europe. She didn't care for the simple Tudor styles prevalent at the beginning of her reign. Instead, she favored everything more exaggerated. Skirts and sleeves were wider, ruffs bigger, and embroidery more ornate. Jewel-encrusted or covered in a rainbow of thread was Queen Elizabeth's kind of gown. By the time she died, the queen had influenced fashion all over England. Even men started wearing girdles, ruffs, and other flamboyant styles.

BORN:
July 14, 1977

HOMETOWN:
Stockholm, Sweden

REGAL BEGINNINGS:
Princess Victoria is the eldest of King Carl XVI Gustaf and Queen Silvia's three children. Sweden has only had three queen regnants in over eight hundred years—when Victoria ascends the throne, she will become the fourth!

PRINCESS OF SWEDEN
VICTORIA

The Royal Life

When Victoria was still a toddler, she became the first female heir to the Swedish throne in three hundred years. Prior to Princess Victoria's birth, Swedish law dictated an agnatic succession, meaning that the throne would be inherited by the first male born to the king and queen. However, this changed in 1979, when the Swedish parliament voted to secure succession rights for the firstborn, regardless of gender, paving the way for Victoria to be the ruler of her country.

ROYAL ACHIEVEMENTS

Victoria has made it a leading goal to become informed in matters of government and international affairs so that she can intelligently represent Sweden. This hasn't always been easy, since Victoria's dyslexia presented a challenge in school. But she worked doubly hard in high school, then attended Yale University, where she studied political science and history. Later she studied conflict resolution in the Diplomat Program at Sweden's Ministry of Foreign Affairs. She didn't stop studying, however, completing internships at the United Nations in New York and the Swedish Embassy in Washington, DC.

ROYALLY COOL FACTS

This princess knows four languages: English, French, German, and—of course—Swedish.

Victoria's hobbies include beekeeping. She's also an avid gardener.

Victoria's favorite animals are horses and dogs—including her Labrador retriever, Jambo.

Crown Princess Victoria with her parents and siblings in 1983. She's the one in the middle.

PRINCESS OF NIGERIA
KEISHA OMILANA

The Royal Life

Before she became a princess, Princess Keisha Omilana was a popular model. In addition to modeling for L'Oreal, Maybelline, Revlon, and Cover Girl, she was the first African American woman to be featured as the "Pantene Girl" in three commercials in a row. But Keisha isn't just a pretty face. She's an actress, too, and has appeared in the movie *Zoolander* and on television in *30 Rock* and *Saturday Night Live.* Her already charmed existence turned into a real-life fairy tale when she met her prince after she became lost on her way to a model casting.

ROYAL ACHIEVEMENTS

Princess Keisha and her husband, Prince Kunle, run Wonderful Media, a company that brings Christian broadcasts to one hundred million homes all over the world. Together they are also helping clergy in building religious communities across Africa.

ROYALLY COOL FACTS

Princess Keisha Omilana is an adventure junkie. She climbed Table Mountain, a flat-topped mountain in South Africa with an elevation of 3,558 feet, in less than an hour!

She didn't find out Kunle was a prince until he asked her to marry him, on Christmas morning!

ROYAL RUNDOWN

BORN:
Unavailable

HOMETOWN:
Inglewood, California

REGAL BEGINNINGS:
Keisha married Prince Kunle Omilana of Nigeria.

DUCHESS OF CAMBRIDGE
KATE

The Royal Life

You just never know where you'll meet Prince Charming. Kate met hers in 2003 while studying art history at the University of St Andrews in Scotland. (Prince William also majored in art history before changing to geography.) They were able to keep their relationship out of the press for more than a year—which is quite an achievement, given the royal-obsessed British paparazzi. But after Kate was seen on a royal family ski trip, life was never common for her again. On April 29, 2011, the former college roomies became the Duke and Duchess of Cambridge when they wed in front of millions of viewers worldwide. Less than a year later, Kate and Will announced they were expecting a baby—and on July 22, 2013, George Alexander Louis arrived. The tyke isn't just adorable—he's also third in line to the throne after his grandpa Prince Charles and his dad, but before his sister, Charlotte Elizabeth Diana, who was born on May 2, 2015, and is fourth in line for the throne.

ROYAL RUNDOWN

BORN:
January 9, 1982

HOMETOWN:
Reading, Berkshire, England

REGAL BEGINNINGS:
Kate and Prince William started their relationship as roommates! Living in an apartment with several other university students, the couple fell in love. Still, they waited eight years to tie the knot and turn Kate from a commoner into a princess.

ROYAL ACHIEVEMENTS

Kate is the ultimate "People's Princess"—a title also bestowed upon William's late mother, Princess Di, for her naturalness and warmth toward others. Even though there isn't a speck of anything royal in Kate's background (she hails from a family of coal miners and builders, although her parents are self-made millionaires), the duchess has never made a misstep in following her royal protocol and duties, which is quite an achievement given so many are tracking her every move. She does find certain aspects of life as a princess stressful—like her wardrobe changes, which can number as many as five a day—and having the secret service and household staff always around. But she's managed to maintain a sense of normalcy, even if it's just putting on her own makeup (which she does) and wearing her dresses more than once (which she also does!). Kate can be spotted at the supermarket, pushing a cart full of groceries like any ordinary mom. Her default evening isn't a grand ball, but a night at home cooking William's favorite dinner of roast chicken and then binge-watching TV.

Kate, one-year-old Prince George, and Will

Kate and Will with their newest royal, Princess Charlotte

ROYALLY
COOL FACTS

Kate's always been a great athlete. She was a member of her university's field hockey team and continues to be an avid tennis player, swimmer, and sailor.

She and William live at Apartment 1A at Kensington Palace. But don't let the word "apartment" throw you. This is a twenty-room property!

In 2012, *Time* magazine named Kate one of the "Most Influential People in the World." Not bad for a thirty-three-year-old.

BORN:
June 9, 1983

HOMETOWN:
London, England

REGAL BEGINNINGS:
Theodora is the youngest of four in a royally blended family. Her father, Constantine II, was King of Greece, and her mother, Anne-Marie, is a Princess of Denmark.

PRINCESS OF GREECE & DENMARK
THEODORA

The Royal Life

Theodora, the goddaughter of Queen Elizabeth, grew up playing with Princes Will and Harry. Their families were incredibly close; Theodora's father is William's godfather, and the godmother of her younger brother was Princess Di. Although she attended three colleges—two in America and one in London—the princess always retained her passion for acting.

ROYALLY COOL FACTS

She started acting in school to overcome her shyness.

In her first acting role, she played Bugsy Malone in a school play—from then on, she was hooked.

ROYAL ACHIEVEMENTS

Theodora has not taken the traditional route of a princess. She is now a professional actress living in Los Angeles, California. Going by her stage name, Theodora Greece, she landed the role of Alison on the long-running soap opera *The Bold and the Beautiful*. Theodora is thrilled to be working on TV, but it did mean she had to miss Prince William's wedding to Kate Middleton. While her parents and brother attended, she had to settle for watching the epic event on TV at 4:00 a.m. back in Los Angeles.

ROYAL HAIRDOS

When wearing a crown, your hair better look good!
Here are some standout styles from well-coiffed queens.

NEFERTITI

This Egyptian queen, famous for her beauty, actually shaved her head with a razor, but she wore Nubian wigs made out of wool, plant fibers, and human hair. During Nefertiti's time, in the mid-1300s BCE, wigs were a fashion statement as well as a symbol of wealth and class. Black silky strands of fake hair reflected the sun and protected the wearer. Nefertiti liked to wear her wig with her favorite crown, a tall, blue, flat-topped one with a gold band, partly because it kept the crown from moving.

MARIE ANTOINETTE

The hairstyles of the last queen of France are legendary. Nothing was off-limits for her hairdresser, Léonard Autié, who could tease the queen's bouffant to a height of nearly four feet. She was known to use her tresses to commemorate important events, like the time Léonard created a look that included a model of a French warship in honor of its sinking a British ship. After she convinced the king to take the smallpox vaccine, she celebrated with the "inoculation pouf," which had a club striking a snake in an olive tree to symbolize the triumph of science. Try brushing out that look!

KATE MIDDLETON

If Marie Antoinette was the definition of high maintenance, then Princess Kate is just the opposite. It doesn't come as a surprise that the princess who prefers to do her own makeup and shop for her own clothes usually wears her hair long, flowing, and natural. You won't find any features, trinkets, or model ships in her bathroom—just a good hair dryer, product to protect her hair from all that heat, and a curling iron for the tips.

AMEERAH AL-TAWEEL

The Royal Life

When eighteen-year-old Ameerah asked to interview one of her country's princes for a school paper, she didn't think her request would be granted. And she certainly didn't think the two would fall in love and marry nine months later. But that's exactly what did happen. The impressive young Saudi woman wed Prince Alwaleed Bin Talal, who isn't just royalty—he's also a billionaire! Equally impressive, the princess graduated magna cum laude from the University of New Haven with a degree in business administration.

ROYAL RUNDOWN

BORN:
November 6, 1983

HOMETOWN:
Riyadh, Saudi Arabia

REGAL BEGINNINGS:
Ameerah, who was raised by her divorced mom and grandparents, married Prince Alwaleed Bin Talal. Unfortunately, it was not happily ever after, since the pair divorced in 2013.

"I didn't want to be that girl who's not doing anything. I wanted to make an impact."

—Ameerah Al-Taweel

ROYAL ACHIEVEMENTS

From the moment she became a princess, Ameerah bucked the traditional role of a Saudi wife by becoming a public figure. She immediately became a strong advocate for women's rights in her country, which are far behind those of men. Part of that was helping to run her husband's charitable foundations, which support many causes—including the empowerment of women. Ameerah has fought hard to pressure Saudi lawmakers to change the laws that don't allow women to drive or to have custody of their children if they get a divorce.

ROYALLY COOL FACTS

Ameerah has taken her fight for the rights of women in the Middle East global, working with many international leaders like former President Bill Clinton and Jordan's Queen Rania.

She has nearly one million Twitter and Instagram followers who she inspires to help her cause.

BORN:
September 1, 1987

HOMETOWN:
Swaziland, Africa

REGAL BEGINNINGS:
Sikhanyiso's father is King
Mswati III of Swaziland,
and her mother is Queen
Inkhosikati LaMbikiza.

PRINCESS OF SWAZILAND
SIKHANYISO

The Royal Life

Sikhanyiso's huge family includes her father, his fourteen wives, twenty-three siblings, and two hundred aunts and uncles (and that's not even including her aunts' and uncles' spouses). Even though she was part of a big brood, she still had her own goals and moved to Australia, where she became a digital communications major at Sydney University. She decided to act just like any ordinary student. She left her servants at home and instead chose to cook and clean for herself while living alone for the very first time. The new experience did present challenges. She had to ask her aunt how to fry an egg!

ROYALLY COOL FACTS

Sikhanyiso doesn't just want to be an activist; she also wants to be a musician. A proud Christian, she is known to belt out a worship song or two. But most of the music she produces is hip-hop, including her song "Hail Your Majesty" about her dad.

ROYAL ACHIEVEMENTS

After graduating, Sikhanyiso returned home to work with various charities based in Africa. Out of all the causes she took up, her political work against polygamy, a tradition in Swaziland, was the bravest. It is the right of every male citizen in her native country to take multiple wives, but as the young princess put it, "Polygamy brings all advantages in a relationship to men, and this to me is unfair and evil." Sikhanyiso was attacked for her strong public statements against this accepted custom. She also defied her father, the king, who with all his wives is clearly a strong supporter of polygamy. Nothing, however, will stop her from speaking out for what she believes in.

Sirivannavari played on the Thai badminton team in the Philippines' 23rd South East Asian Games in 2005.

The princess was the December 2014 cover girl for *Harper's Bazaar* Thailand.

PRINCESS OF THAILAND
SIRIVANNAVARI

The Royal Life

When Sirivannavari was ten years old, her parents split up. That's hard enough on any child, but for the young Thai princess it had an impact of royal proportions. The divorce meant her mother lost her title—and her citizenship! No longer part of the royal family, Sirivannavari's mother was forced to leave Thailand for England, along with her young children. But when Sirivannavari turned eighteen, her father demanded she return to Thailand. On July 15, 2005, her grandfather, the king, officially restored her status as a princess.

ROYAL RUNDOWN

BORN:
January 8, 1987

HOMETOWN:
Bangkok, Thailand

REGAL BEGINNINGS:
Sirivannavari Nariatana's name translates to "the Royal Granddaughter" in honor of her grandparents, King Bhumibol Adulyadej and Queen Sirikit of Thailand. Sirivannavari's father is Crown Prince Maha Vajiralongkorn, and her mother is Sujarinee Vivacharawongse, also known as Yuvadhida Polpraserth.

Princess Sirivannavari riding dressage at the 2014 Incheon Asian Games

ROYAL ACHIEVEMENTS

Sirivannavari is a fabulous fashion designer! In 2008, she was invited to Paris Fashion Week to present her debut collection, which was a modern take on traditional Thai clothing. Her clothes were so good that the following year, she had her own fashion show in Paris. But Sirivannavari's newer designs are anything but traditional, with a spandex dress and metallic bell-bottoms. Sirivannavari is also an accomplished athlete, and has called her clothing "remarkable sports couture."

PRINCESSES OF YORK
BEATRICE AND EUGENIE

The Royal Life

Other than the fact that "Granny" is Her Majesty the Queen, Beatrice and Eugenie are known as normal people who don't expect royal treatment from anyone. Eugenie is so down-to-earth that she loves hot dogs and rides the subway! Beatrice, meanwhile, is open about the fact that she's not perfect, and faced a lot of difficulty in school because of her dyslexia. Another normal fact about the princesses? They fight over clothes just like many sisters!

Princess Beatrice

Princess Eugenie

The royals and their mom at a wedding in 1993

ROYAL ACHIEVEMENTS

Beatrice is a charity machine! She has followed her mother's example by becoming a global ambassador for Children in Crisis, a foundation to educate women and children in poor countries, which her mother started in 1993. Beatrice is also the patron of six foundations that help sick children and support struggling communities. Princess Eugenie is a patron of the Royal National Orthopaedic Hospital, a cause that stems from personal experience: She struggled with scoliosis as a child and had corrective surgery at age twelve.

"How do I play the princess thing? I don't really."

—Princess Eugenie

ROYALLY COOL FACTS

Of those in line for the throne, Beatrice is the second female on the list!

Beatrice appeared in the film *The Young Victoria*, portraying one of her great-great-great-great grandmother's ladies-in-waiting.

Eugenie is a fan of the TV show *Big Brother*, the indie music band Death Cab for Cutie, and the American artist Jean-Michel Basquiat.

PRINCE CHARMING

After reading about all these inspiring princesses, are you ready to don a tiara of your own? Well, there are still a few eligible princes around . . .

PRINCE HARRY

Okay, Harry the redheaded royal, fourth in line for the British throne, might sometimes be known more for his partying than anything else. But Harry isn't all about fun. He's not only fought on the front lines in Afghanistan as part of Britain's army but he also does a variety of charity work and has made a documentary about AIDS—a subject that was important to his late mother, Princess Diana.

94

PRINCE PHILIPPOS

As the son of the former King of Greece (the country no longer has a monarchy), Philippos is a royal by blood alone. But that doesn't make him any less dreamy. The Georgetown University graduate is so reserved that he turned down an offer to star in his own reality show.

HUSSEIN BIN ABDULLAH

The Crown Prince of Jordan decided to major in political science at Georgetown University. Although he might be brainy, he still has his wild side. Like his dad, Prince Abdullah is really into riding motorcycles.

PRINCE ALBERT VON THURN UND TAXIS

This German aristocrat might have no constitutional power to rule, but he's got a lot of cash! The race car driver is said to be worth $1.5 billion, earning him a spot on the *Forbes* "World's Youngest Billionaires" list.

PHOTO CREDITS